A Tree Sleep

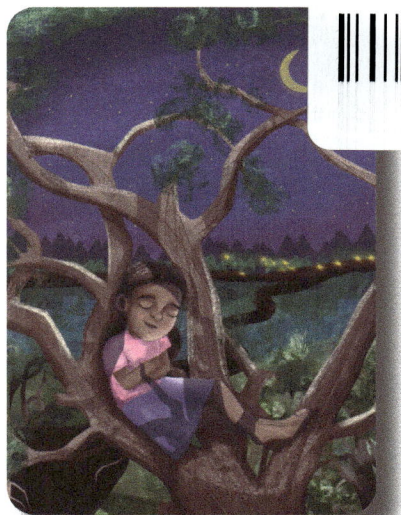

By Lila Cairns
From Doomadgee Community, Queensland

Library For All Ltd.

Library For All is an Australian not for profit organisation with a mission to make knowledge accessible to all via an innovative digital library solution. Visit us at libraryforall.org

A Tree Sleep

First published 2023

Published by Library For All Ltd
Email: info@libraryforall.org
URL: libraryforall.org

Library For All gratefully acknowledges the contributions of all who made previous editions of this book possible.

This edition made possible by the generous contributions of GSK and 54 reasons.

Our Yarning logo design by Jason Lee, Bidjipidji Art

Original illustrations by Mila Aydingoz

A Tree Sleep
Cairns, Lila
ISBN: 978-1-922991-92-8
SKU01373

A Tree Sleep

Lila, with her mum and cousin, went hunting for bush bananas, conkerberries, and goanna.

It was hot and Lila wore her new Christmas present, a lovely petticoat.

Lila left her petticoat by the path and forgot to grab it when her mum and cousin kept going for goanna.

Mum called her, but Lila wanted her present.

Lila went back to find her new petticoat. Soon, she was a long way from her mum.

She called out and looked for footprints, but she was lost.

She walked and walked until she heard a pack of dingoes close by.

She knew she had to get up a tree to be safe, so she climbed as high as she could.

Lila was high up and saw headlights in the west. She knew that was the way to the main road and got comfortable in the tree, safe.

In the morning, Lila climbed down from her safe sleeping place and started to walk to the main road.

She was tired and hungry.

Lila's big brothers and cousins were driving around looking for her.

As they drove past, Lila called out.

One of her cousins saw her, and they stopped the car to pick her up.

They all laughed at her tree sleep adventure and took her back to her mum and dad.

Everybody was so pleased to see her safe and unharmed.

Her mum smiled as she handed her the lost petticoat.

Her family had been so worried for her.

Lila learnt her lesson:
don't leave Mum when out
hunting and always listen to
grown-ups to stay safe.

You can use these questions to talk about this book with your family, friends and teachers.

What did you learn from this book?

Describe this book in one word. Funny? Scary? Colourful? Interesting?

How did this book make you feel when you finished reading it?

What was your favourite part of this book?

download our reader app
getlibraryforall.org

Hello Readers!

In 2021, Save The Children Australia and Library For All worked with the Doomadgee community to develop a children's book series. The stories were written in English and translated into Gangalidda, Garrawa and Waanyi, three of the most widely spoken languages in the region. Beautiful illustrations and engaging photos were selected to ensure these books encourage children to learn to read, and love to read, while celebrating culture and country.

Our Yarning

Want to discover more books from this collection? Our Yarning is a collection of books written by Aboriginal and Torres Strait Islander peoples across Australia.

We know that children learn better, and enjoy reading more, when they see themselves in the stories, characters and illustrations of the books they read.

To download the app, visit the Google Play Store on any Android device and search 'Our Yarning'.